You're a Pal, Snoopy!

by Charles M. Schulz

Selected cartoons from
You Need Help, Charlie Brown, Volume 2

A FAWCETT CREST BOOK

Fawcett Publications, Inc., Greenwich, Conn.

Other Peanuts Books in Fawcett Crest Editions
Include the Following:

YOU'VE DONE IT AGAIN, CHARLIE BROWN D1441
  (selected cartoons from We're Right Behind You,
  Charlie Brown, Vol. 2)

IT'S FOR YOU, SNOOPY   D1559
  (selected cartoons from Sunday's Fun Day,
  Charlie Brown, Vol. 1)

HAVE IT YOUR WAY, CHARLIE BROWN   D1572
  (selected cartoons from Sunday's Fun Day,
  Charlie Brown, Vol. 2)

YOU'RE NOT FOR REAL, SNOOPY   D1622
  (selected cartoons from You Need Help,
  Charlie Brown, Vol. 1)

Only 50¢ Each—Wherever Paperbacks Are Sold

If your bookdealer is sold out, send cover price plus 15¢
each for postage and handling to Mail Order Department,
Fawcett Publications, Inc., Greenwich, Connecticut 06830.
Please order by number and title. No Canadian orders.
Catalog available on request.

MY HEART IS FULL ON THE DAY I FIRST GO OUT TO THE OL' BALL FIELD...

AH! THERE IT IS! MY PITCHER'S MOUND...COVERED WITH TRADITION..

I LOVE THE SMELL OF THE HORSEHIDE, THE GRASSY OUTFIELD AND THE DUSTY INFIELD...I LOVE THE MEMORIES..THE HOPES...AND THE DREAMS FOR THE NEW SEASON..

AND DANDELIONS!

WHAT IN THE WORLD ARE ALL THESE DANDELIONS DOING ON THE PITCHER'S MOUND?

THEY **GREW** THERE! AND MY STUPID GIRL-OUTFIELDERS WON'T LET ME CUT THEM DOWN! THEY SAY THEY'RE PRETTY, AND I LOOK **CUTE** STANDING HERE AMONG THEM!

THEY'RE RIGHT...YOU **DO** LOOK KIND OF CUTE STANDING THERE..

SCHULZ

PTUI!

I MUST ADMIT I HAVE THE MOST UNIQUE DOUBLE-PLAY COMBINATION IN BASEBALL!

I WROTE A LETTER FOR SNOOPY TO THE DAISY HILL PUPPY FARM..

I HOPE THEY ANSWER RIGHT AWAY BECAUSE HE'S PRETTY EXCITED...HE WANTS TO TRY TO FIND HIS BROTHERS AND SISTERS...

I SUPPOSE HE'S WAITING RIGHT BY THE MAILBOX...

YES, I THINK YOU COULD SAY THAT..

YOU'RE GETTING PRETTY GOOD ON THAT SKATEBOARD, LINUS!

BUT HE CAN'T DO "WHEELIES"!

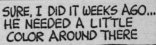

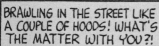

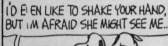

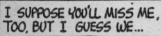

ROY, YOU'VE GOT TO SNAP OUT OF IT!

A CAMP LIKE THIS IS THE BEST PLACE FOR SOMEONE LIKE YOU...IT HELPS YOU TO BREAK THOSE OLD APRON STRINGS!

LIFE IS FULL OF EXPERIENCES THAT HAVE TO BE FACED ALONE!

BUT YOU SAID YOU WERE LONESOME, TOO..

I TALK A GOOD CAMP...

DEAR MOM AND DAD,
THINGS ARE GOING
BETTER HERE AT CAMP.

Yesterday I met
this kid named
Charlie Brown.

HE WAS VERY LONESOME,
BUT I THINK I HAVE
HELPED HIM.

He's the kind who
makes a good
temporary friend.

STRIKE THREE!

WHAT'S THE MATTER, KID? AIN'TCHA NEVER PLAYED BASEBALL BEFORE?!!

WHY DIDN'T YOU TELL HIM, CHARLIE BROWN? WHY DIDN'T YOU TELL HIM ABOUT HOW YOU'RE THE MANAGER OF A TEAM AT HOME?

SOMEHOW, MENTIONING A TEAM THAT HAS THREE GIRL-OUTFIELDERS AND A DOG-SHORTSTOP DIDN'T SEEM QUITE APPROPRIATE!

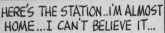

STRIKE ONE!

OOOOOO! C'MON, CHARLIE BROWN, **HIT IT**! FOR ONCE IN YOUR LIFE, **HIT IT**!!

WOULDN'T YOU LIKE JUST FOR ONCE TO SEE CHARLIE BROWN HIT THAT BALL?

NO..

I'M NOT PREPARED TO HAVE THE WORLD COME TO AN END!

SCHULZ

PERHAPS YOU SHOULDN'T BE A PLAYING MANAGER, CHARLIE BROWN...PERHAPS YOU SHOULD BE A BENCH MANAGER..

THAT'S A GOOD IDEA... YOU'D BE A GREAT BENCH MANAGER, CHARLIE BROWN...

YOU COULD SAY, "BENCH, DO THIS! BENCH, DO THAT!" YOU COULD EVEN BE IN CHARGE OF WHERE WE PUT THE BENCH..

WHEN THE TEAM GETS TO THE BALL PARK, YOU COULD SAY, "LET'S PUT THE BENCH HERE!" OR, "LET'S PUT THE BENCH THERE!"

I CAN'T STAND IT!

THERE'S A RUMOR GOING AROUND THAT I WON'T BE PLAYING ANY MORE..

WELL, I'M NOT QUITTING BASEBALL JUST BECAUSE I GOOFED A FEW TIMES! I'M STILL THE MANAGER OF THIS TEAM, AND WHAT I SAY GOES!

NOW, THERE'S STILL TIME LEFT IN THIS SEASON FOR US TO MAKE A GOOD SHOWING IF WE'LL ALL JUST GRIT OUR TEETH, AND..

SCHULZ

SHOW-TIME AGAIN! ≿SIGH≾

EVERY SATURDAY AFTERNOON I GO TO THE SHOW...IT'S SURPRISING HOW QUICKLY THE WEEKS GO BY WHEN YOU DO THE SAME THING EVERY SATURDAY

I SHOULD DO SOMETHING DIFFERENT

IT'S MAKING MY LIFE GO BY TOO FAST!

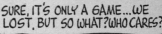

PIG-PEN, YOU ARE A PERPETUAL MESS...

I CAN TELL JUST WHERE YOU'VE BEEN ALL WEEK FROM THE DIRT ON YOUR CLOTHES...YESTERDAY YOU WERE DOWN BY THE TRAIN TRACKS..

YOU SPENT THE DAY BEFORE DOWN AT THE PLAYGROUND, THE DUMP AND THE WAREHOUSE..

I DON'T HAVE TO LISTEN TO THIS..

AND MONDAY YOU SPENT ALL DAY AT THE BRICK YARD, ISN'T THAT RIGHT?

SCHULZ

WHY AREN'T YOU A PONY?!!

WHY DID YOU WRITE, "CHARLIE BROWN IS A BLOCKHEAD" ON THE SIDEWALK?

BECAUSE I SINCERELY BELIEVE YOU ARE A BLOCKHEAD! I HAVE TO WRITE WHAT I BELIEVE IS TRUE.. IT'S MY MORAL RESPONSIBILITY!

DEEP DOWN I ADMIRE HER INTEGRITY..

LISTEN TO THIS..

IT SAYS HERE THAT BY 1980 THERE WILL BE A NEED FOR 47,250 VETERINARIANS...

BUT IT ALSO SAYS THAT THERE WILL BE A SHORTAGE OF OVER 8000 VETERINARIANS...

REMIND ME NOT TO BE SICK IN 1980 !

SCHULZ

DEAR PENCIL-PAL,
HAVE YOU HAD A
NICE SUMMER?

I LIKE TO READ, DO YOU?
I AM VERY FOND OF BOOKS.

I CAN ALWAYS ENJOY A
GOOD BOOK. I HAVE ALWAYS
BEEN THE SORT OF PERSON
WHO ENJOYS READING.

WHEN I HAVE NOTHING
ELSE TO DO, I READ.

SCHULZ

HOMEWORK ALREADY! WRITE A THOUSAND-WORD ESSAY ON WHAT WE DID DURING THE SUMMER!

NOBODY CAN WRITE A THOUSAND-WORD ESSAY ON WHAT HE DID DURING THE SUMMER! IT'S RIDICULOUS!

WHEN ARE YOU GOING TO TRY TO WRITE YOURS. THIS EVENING?

MINE'S ALREADY FINISHED. I WROTE IT DURING STUDY PERIOD!

YOU DRIVE ME CRAZY!!!

SCHULZ

DO YOU KNOW WHY ENGLISH TEACHERS GO TO COLLEGE FOR FOUR YEARS?

NO, I DON'T KNOW WHY ENGLISH TEACHERS GO TO COLLEGE FOR FOUR YEARS..

WELL THEN I'LL TELL YOU WHY ENGLISH TEACHERS GO TO COLLEGE FOR FOUR YEARS....

SO THEY CAN MAKE STUPID LITTLE KIDS WRITE STUPID ESSAYS ON WHAT THEY DID ALL STUPID SUMMER!!

I WONDER IF THERE ARE "PEOPLE" STARS AND "DOG" STARS?

DEAR GREAT PUMPKIN, SOMETHING HAS OCCURRED TO ME.

YOU MUST GET DISCOURAGED BECAUSE MORE PEOPLE BELIEVE IN SANTA CLAUS THAN IN YOU.

WELL, LET'S FACE IT... SANTA CLAUS HAS HAD MORE PUBLICITY.

BUT BEING NUMBER TWO, PERHAPS YOU TRY HARDER.

SCHULZ

DEAR GREAT PUMPKIN, YOU'VE MADE A FOOL OUT OF ME FOR THE LAST TIME! I'M REALLY GOING TO TELL YOU OFF.

DON'T BURN ALL OF YOUR BRIDGES BEHIND YOU...

SIGH!

SCHULZ

ONLY 6 DAYS UNTIL BEETHOVEN'S BIRTHDAY

ELEVEN DAYS TO THE FIRST DAY OF WINTER

ONLY 12 SHOPPING DAYS UNTIL CHRISTMAS

IT'S UNUSUAL FOR ONE AGENCY TO HAVE ALL THREE ACCOUNTS!

NOW Peanuts Jewelry

Each item is 14 Kt. gold finish, hand-crafted cloisonné in brilliant colors, exquisitely designed by Aviva. Items shown in actual size. Complete satisfaction guaranteed or money refunded.

No. 10 pin $3

No. 11 pin $3

No. 12 pin $3

No. 13A pierced $3
No. 13B non-pierced $3

No. 14 pin $3

No. 15 pin $3

No. 16 pin $3

No. 17A pierced $3
No. 17B non-pierced $3

No. 18 pin $3

No. 19 pin $3

No. 20 pin $3

© United Feature Syndicate, Inc. 1971

No. 21 pin $3

More Peanuts Jewelry
See Previous Page

No. 22 tie tack $3

No. 23 tie tack $3

No. 24 key chain $3

No. 25 money clip $4

No. 26 tie tack $3

No. 27 tie bar $3

No. 28 cufflinks $4

No. 29 pin $3

Please specify identity number of each item
ordered and add 25¢ for each item to cover
postage and handling. Personal check or
money order. No cash. Send orders to
HAMILTON HOUSE, Cos Cob, Conn. 06807.
© United Feature Syndicate, Inc. 1971